DOGS & DEVOTION

The photo credits on p. 95 constitute a continuation of this copyright page.

Library of Congress Cataloging-in-Publication Data

Dogs & devotion / the Monks of New Skete. -- 1st ed.
p. cm.
ISBN 978-1-4013-2296-0
1. Dogs--Behavior. 2. Dogs--Psychology. 3. Dogs--Psychological
aspects. 4. Human-animal relationships. I. Monks of New Skete. II.
Title: Dogs and devotion.
SF433.D65 2008
636.7--dc22   2008053369

Hyperion books are available for special promotions and premiums.
For details contact the HarperCollins Special Markets Department in the New York
office at 212-207-7528, Fax 212-207-7222, or email spsales@harpercollins.com.

First Edition

10 9 8 7 6 5 4 3 2 1

DOGS & DEVOTION

THE MONKS OF NEW SKETE

NEW YORK

INTRODUCTION

To a significant degree, the commitments we make in life define us. They reveal our interests, passions and goals, and give important clues in discerning meaning and finding happiness in life. While many seem to struggle with the archetypal human question, "who am I?" one simple look at who and what you're devoted to, what takes up your time and fires your imagination can clarify your life direction. It can help you to make authentic decisions that are rooted in your deepest convictions. We are happiest when we are in harmony with our passion.

Interestingly, the connections we have with the animal world, especially with our dogs, have an important role to play in our growth and self-understanding. Put simply, we don't hide in front of our dogs: we see ourselves as we really are. Whether it involves the love and generosity of spirit expressed in getting our dog necessary and expensive medical treatment, or experiencing our uncontrolled anger erupting over an accident on the carpet, dogs have the capacity of bringing out the light and dark in human nature. By taking such moments of personal insight seriously, we have a daily touchstone with reality: we can change and grow. Perhaps one of the reasons we are so devoted to our dogs is that they help us become who we're supposed to be.

Monks have always had an essential connection with devotion; we cannot but delight in recognizing God's mystery in the length and breadth of daily life. In our particular monastic context of New Skete, we have been privileged to share this in a special way with our German Shepherds, who in an entirely natural way have taught us many important lessons about life and about ourselves. Some of these are what we share with you in the following meditations, hoping that they might be the occasion for a taste of more abundant life.

Perhaps one of the reasons we are
so devoted to our dogs is that they help us
become who we're supposed to be.

"A LOYAL FRIEND IS A POWERFUL
DEFENSE: WHOEVER FINDS ONE
HAS INDEED FOUND A TREASURE.
A LOYAL FRIEND IS SOMETHING
BEYOND PRICE, THERE IS NO
MEASURING HIS WORTH. A LOYAL
FRIEND IS THE ELIXIR OF LIFE."

~ Ecclesiastes 6:14-16

PATHWAYS TO THE SOUL

How easy to get lost in a dog's eyes!

They are the pathways to its soul, orbs that help us realize the depth of good will and devotion that are ours at a moment's notice. They reveal sentiments that are focused and sincere, beyond doubt and questioning. A dog's eyes do not lie. When we catch the gaze of our best friend, there is no shame, no embarrassment, only the sheer transparency of a creature who can't possibly deceive and whose love can never be merited.

ENGAGEMENT

Is there anything more irresistible
than a dog soliciting play?

You can see it in their eyes: the delight, the hint of mischief, the complete focus. Dogs throw themselves wholeheartedly into play with a transparency that can teach us if we pay attention. Dogs have no time for apathy, for ennui. Do you seek to live fully, energized by being engaged with the things you love? Give yourself as passionately to life as a dog does to its play and see how your life will be transformed.

THE WHOLEHEARTED LIFE

Nothing so captures the uninhibited, spontaneous
nature of a dog as when it rolls on its back and
becomes one with whatever scent has struck its fancy.

Back and forth, to and fro, its spirit radiates through
the sheer enjoyment of this private ritual. Is not
this one of the traits that so endears us to our dogs,
even when their choice of scent is beyond our
comprehension? Whatever they do, dogs usually
do it wholeheartedly, with no embarrassment or
shame. For them, life is simply one successive
enchantment after another, to be recognized and
acted upon day after day after day.

POSSIBILITY

Perhaps the most enchanting
> quality of a puppy is possibility.

Puppies fill us with hope, giving us a chance to start over again, to shape them and ourselves into long-term companions who will share an intimate part of each other's lives for the next ten to twenty years.

"JUST A DOG."

Part of the wonder of a life with
dogs is their incredible diversity.

Not only do different breeds display distinctive looks and characteristics, but the individuals themselves vary in so many intriguing and unusual ways that transcend the particular breed. Quite simply put, dogs are fascinating. Over time, one's appreciation and love for dogs expand as the mystery of individual personalities manifests itself, making us realize how far from the mark the unflattering characterization "but it's just a dog" really is. In fact, there is no such thing as "just a dog."

SPIRIT

Dogs possess an indomitable
spirit for life that teaches right
up to their last day.

It is as if they stubbornly refuse to concede that
life can be anything other than a gift to which
they must respond. The wagging tail gives it
away: Even an illness as serious as cancer has no
effect on them when a favorite ball is involved...
at least for a while. The focus remains fixed, and
the usual enthusiasm will be manifest until they
can simply push themselves no longer. They
won't let go until every worthwhile moment
of life is sucked dry. Therein lies their nobility:
Dogs are an homage to life.

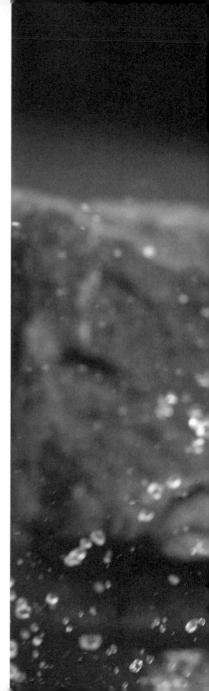

FAMILY DOG.

Dogs love so unambiguously, so unapologetically,
that often some of our deepest experiences of
love as children come in relationship to a dog.

The devoted family dog does not stop to wonder whether a lick
is appropriate. It simply manifests it spontaneously, and children
are immediately aware of its honest sincerity. There is nothing
manipulative about it, and children don't doubt it for a second.
Its meaning is clear: love – no strings attached.

NO FENCES

Dogs don't seem to like fences.

The very presence of a barrier often elicits a fury of protectiveness that otherwise wouldn't be manifest. A dog barking wildly behind a fence one moment can easily turn into a friendly pooch the next: All that is necessary is the dropping of the barrier. Not always, but frequently. Might we not glean a lesson from this? At the very least, the barrier we bark behind can sabotage the depth we seek with those we love. Drop the barrier and a new level of relationship and trust might occur.

THE HAPPY DOG.

Dogs place such modest
            conditions on their happiness.

Companionship, a requirement of their social nature; adequate food and
water to replenish their bodies and allow them to energetically engage
with life; and ample periods for rest and relaxation, as a balance for
their more vigorous activities. These "essentials" satisfy the wide spectrum
of happy canines who seamlessly adapt to the changing conditions of
everyday life. It is not that dogs don't love other things such as digging
holes for bones or taking a ride in the car, but these and countless other
activities are icing on the cake, frills that build on an already solid

contentment. In a world whose
complexity and demands seem to
escalate without our even realizing it,
we do well to take note of our dogs,
who always manage to keep their
priorities in place and who are able
to enter fully into the moment.

ABBA XANTHIAS SAID,
"A DOG IS BETTER THAN I AM,
FOR HE HAS LOVE AND DOES NOT JUDGE."

~ The Sayings of the Desert Fathers

DOG AS THERAPIST

Dogs know instinctively how to get us
out of our emotional doldrums – all
they have to do is stick to their script.

In the midst of their antics – if we pay attention – our depression and
self-pity can be swallowed up by canine spontaneity and joy. Before
we know it, a smile has replaced a grimace. What a gift! We may
try to fight their charms and hold on to our misery but, in the end,
resistance is futile. Their infectious zest and passion for
life are simply too much for whatever bad mood
seems to be hobbling us.

SIMPLICITY AND DOGS

Dogs are intensely curious about the world
they live in, and they investigate its breadth
relentlessly with all their senses.

Checking out an irresistible scent in the grass captivates them as much
as gnawing at a treasured bone in the yard. Simple activities, perhaps,
yet dogs engage in them with a relish and single-minded focus from
which we can draw inspiration. One of the real secrets of a peaceful
and happy life is to be grateful for the small things that daily come
our way: a fresh cup of coffee, a conversation with a friend, a jog
through our neighborhood. Dogs teach spontaneously through the
joy they find close to home.

SIMPLE PLEASURES

Can we exhaust the inspiration
to be drawn from the creative
nature of the dog?

Dogs manage to tease mischief and joy out of
the most modest of circumstances. Unlike their
human counterparts, whose needs seem to
have no ceiling, dogs are content with simple
pleasures: chasing a ball, a walk in the woods,
evening supper … and they revel in these with
unabashed enthusiasm. In the dog's eye, reality
is purely an opportunity for engagement, a
date it never fails to meet.

THE LONG HAUL

The word "companion" means, literally, "sharing bread," and while ordinarily we don't share our food with our dogs, we do experience a unique intimacy with them that has withstood the test of time.

Dogs and human beings have been journeying together for over fifteen thousand years, helping each other in ways that are astonishing considering they take place between different species. We have both evolved to the point where we are in this relationship together for the long haul, and it is endlessly fascinating to witness the new ways this companionship expresses itself.

FAITH

It may seem surprising to associate faith with our bond with a dog, but truly it's an essential component.

Faith helps us believe in what is possible, in how deep we can go with the relationship. Each dog is unique, and a good relationship adapts intuitively to the temperament and needs of the particular dog who shares our life. There are likely to be some rough spots where things don't seem to be going as expected and where we can start doubting ourselves. But believing in the process, and having faith in the wisdom of those who have worked with all manner of dogs, can help us relax and listen closely to the needs of the moment, and respond appropriately.

DO NOT JUDGE

A wonderful character trait of dogs is
         their lack of judging us in a critical way.

The strong bonds that come with a dog's companionship go
beyond externals, connecting with deeper realities that lie
beneath surface appearances. The fierce devotion of a dog to
a down-and-out street person is only one example among many
of how dogs can recognize what most others overlook. Dogs have
no trouble seeing the best parts of ourselves; what would it be
like if we actually believed them?

LEGACY AND LONGEVITY

One secret of deepening any sort of relationship with
our dogs is giving them time to develop and age.

This is especially the case with young dogs. By keeping in mind the
dog's reality as a unique, developing creature, we can avoid applying
excessive pressure that might cause it to react with less self-confidence
and trust than we would desire. By patiently allowing the dog's
personality to blossom, and cooperating with that process, we have
a better chance of seeing its capacity as a companion and friend
realized in a legacy of fidelity and joy.

HONORING RELATIONSHIPS

In a fractured world of broken relationships dogs
can teach us the meaning of devotion and fidelity.

Dogs honor their relationships. They don't opt out
when things don't go their way, but manage to
adjust to the alternating climates of everyday life.
They sway according to our moods, and intuitively
know when to approach and solicit attention. We
can learn a lesson about how to negotiate our own
human relationships by observing this dynamic in
our dogs, who seem to understand instinctively
how to respond to us in whatever way we need.

DOGS AT THE CENTER

Dogs can't help themselves: By simply being who they are they cast a spell on our attention that lets them find a place at the center of our universe.

As they spontaneously draw out different dimensions of ourselves – some that may be hidden even from us – they become doorways to deeper self-knowledge and wholeness that renew and refresh us. Being alive to this puts the ordinary responsibilities associated with caring for a dog in a new perspective, one less of inconvenience than of privilege.

WHAT DOES LOVE LOOK LIKE?

Whatever loving a dog may mean,
　　　　it doesn't mean indulging it in a way that spoils.

Extreme pampering is a trap whose only logic is to
make us feel good. It doesn't serve the dog in the least.
True companionship and the love that is its driving
force are characterized by taking the dog's true needs
into account, and doing our level best to meet them.
Long walks, vigorous exercise, and the companionship
that comes with these are much more to the point than
cramming extra calories at meal times. Not only will
your dog love you for it, you'll be extending the years
you can enjoy each other.

"THERE IS LITTLE THAT SEPARATES
HUMANS FROM OTHER SENTIENT
BEINGS — WE ALL FEEL PAIN, WE
ALL FEEL JOY, WE ALL DEEPLY
CRAVE TO BE ALIVE AND LIVE
FREELY, AND WE ALL SHARE
THIS PLANET TOGETHER."

~ Gandhi

TRAINING

In a relationship with a dog, who trains whom?
Often we assume training is a one-dimensional
activity that expresses dominance over a
subordinate in a fairly straightforward manner.

While healthy leadership is a vital part of any
successful relationship between human and dog,
to the watchful eye real training happens
differently. There is a reciprocal flow of information
in the training process that not only teaches the
dog, but teaches us as well, if we're attentive to
the moment. Dare we overlook such bits of self-
knowledge? Dogs continuously reflect back to us
all that we communicate to them – either their
understanding or lack thereof. When we
understand this positively, the possibility for
personal transformation is as close as the
relationship we form with them.

READING THE DOG

At the foundation of our enchantment with dogs is the capacity for experiencing relationship – particularly the fascination that occurs when we transcend the species boundary and truly communicate with dogs as fellow creatures.

What worlds open up for us when we connect on this level, the wonder that erupts almost effortlessly! Dogs are speaking all the time, if we understand speech in broader terms than simply human communication. To take such "speech" to the levels that are possible, we have to have a disciplined and practiced eye, a heart that reads the language inscribed on the dog's body. From the erect tail and ears, bristling with attention, to the wagging tail that solicits play, to the piercing eyes that exert dominance: All have deep significance in the canine lexicon. One of the most serious responsibilities from our end of the relationship is to be ever mindful of what the dog is saying and alert to a proper response.

GRACEFUL DOGS

Sometimes dogs fit so effortlessly within our landscape
that we actually forget they are around – we take
them for granted, thoughtlessly consigning them to
the margins of our attention without taking into
account their own needs as unique creatures.

We get so lost in our own concerns that we forget the legitimate place they fill in
our lives, losing touch with their stabilizing, humanizing influence. They sense
this, naturally, but rarely reciprocate with moodiness and distance. Instead,
they think up ingenious ways of re-entering our lives, soliciting our attention,
pulling our play strings, helping us re-establish a certain balance and
equilibrium with the everyday that keeps us grounded and sane.

PATIENCE

Often when we adopt a new puppy, we have a
  vision of the type of relationship we hope for.

Based, in part, on past experiences, or on what we
have read about or witnessed with friends, we can
easily put more pressure on ourselves and on the
pup than is wise. Patience is a key virtue in
nurturing the relationship, to keep us relaxed and
moving forward step by step. With patience we can
stay in touch with the bigger picture, realizing that
the foundations of a healthy relationship are laid
over a broad period of time. No relationship of any
real depth matures overnight – human or canine;
trusting in the process will give us a calmness and
flexibility in the face of challenges that arise
naturally from time to time.

DOG DAYS

Dogs always seem to know when to be lazy.

They can lean into a relaxed moment and nurse it to the full, savoring it without an ounce of guilt or regret, seemingly dead to the world. But how quickly the mood shifts the second something of interest tracks on their radar … like a squirrel racing across the yard. In an instant they're all attention: ears, eyes and nose conspiring effortlessly to respond to the drama of the moment, never second-guessing themselves to wonder whether it's worth the energy. The dog engages totally, energy married to its reward. But not for long: Before you know it, the cycle soon repeats itself, the dog returning to its posture of rest and waiting, waiting for the next squirrel to test its vigilance.

61

GRACE

Think "dog" and what spontaneously arises in
the mind is most often the loyalty and devotion
they express towards us, sometimes in the most
remarkable of circumstances.

Innumerable tales of rescue, comfort, and healing confirm that their
connection with us is more than human projection; it's a grace we
could never merit. That said, our devotion to them seems much more
than a simple quid pro quo proposition. Dogs enchant something
deep in human nature and we have been striving to build on this for
thousands of years through breeding and companionship. Where
does that come from? Indeed, dogs have elicited the love, care, and
concern that reflect the best of us.

DOGS ARE AWESOME

Precisely because dogs are so common in our society,
we may overlook how awesome they are as a species.

Individual members of *Canis familiaris* may indeed reside in every town, city, or rural landscape, but their collective talents reflect gifts that are able to adapt to an infinite variety of situations for our benefit. That fact alone should inspire us to seek the most humane and enlightened ways of sharing their companionship. But this need not be our sole motive. Let us understand that being a good companion affects our moral character as well. Aside from helping us in hunting, law enforcement, farm work, and human assistance, to name only a few, dogs help us to become better human beings, more alive to the connections we have with the universe and grateful for the consciousness of that communion.

ON BEING ADAPTABLE

Dogs teach us an important
lesson by easily adapting to the
changing circumstances of life.

Their happiness isn't contingent on always
getting their way. No matter how their natural
preferences get "detoured," they effortlessly
make the best of whatever comes up without
complaint. A "no" on the comfortable couch?
They easily flop on the floor, almost acting as if
it were their idea. The fluctuations of weather?
Dogs are able to enjoy whatever Mother Nature
throws at them without a lot of fuss: Rain or
shine, they will figure out the best way to enjoy
the walk. What could be more reasonable?

DIGGING FOR TREASURE

Most dogs love to dig. Theories abound as
        to why, but the simple fact is that something
                under the surface is attracting them:

the prospect of a cool den on a hot day, for example, or a hidden
treasure that only they can detect. Whatever the reason, dogs don't
go about this tentatively. A dog digging is engaged, and can be an
illuminating metaphor for us regarding our own inner work. We don't
get beneath the surface of our lives unless we put heart and soul into
the effort. But if we choose to, what rich discoveries we make!

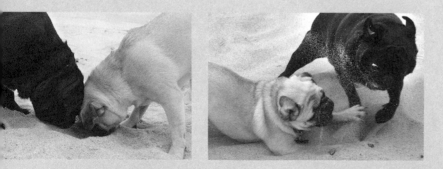

LEADERSHIP

For the human/dog relationship to blossom, dogs
    require leadership from their human companions.

As pack animals, dogs are instinctively sensitive to social hierarchies
and function beautifully when they understand their place in the pack.
Nevertheless, the way we conceive of leadership is crucial if this principle
is to hold true. Leadership is not arbitrary domination or a craving for
power. More than anything, when we assume a role of leadership with
our dogs, we must recognize our responsibility in helping the dog achieve
its potential at the same time that it relishes its own fulfillment. How
rich the possibilities!

*"O Creator and Maker of
all things, through your Holy
Spirit always present in our
midst, bless our animals, pets,
and companions, and keep
them safe from every harm
and disrespect."*

~ Feast of St Francis of Assisi,
The Blessing of the Animals

CONNECTION

At a time when human nature is being stretched by
all sorts of competing pressures, the presence of dogs
in our lives helps to keep us sane and balanced.

Dogs are a touchstone to a more primal wisdom that points to the
importance of being connected to other beings – human beings to be
sure, but other creatures as well. We don't find happiness filling our
loneliness with the empty promises of "things." Our connection with
dogs helps us identify priorities, honoring the personal in favor of
more materialistic expectations society seems so often to prefer.

DOGS ENRICH US

While we are vividly conscious of how dogs
enrich human life, we seldom consider that
dogs also have made a deliberate choice
to associate with human beings.

Put simply, our presence has been advantageous
to them, not only in acquiring regular food, but
in obtaining emotional support and protection as
well. Recognizing this offers us a daily opportunity
for growth, a transcending of our own limited ego
concerns. Out of their need, dogs call our best
selves forward, challenging us to a sense of
responsibility and commitment that builds with
each passing day. From such a perspective, daily
chores play an important role in our own
transformation.

INQUISITIVENESS

Dogs try to figure us out all the time.

We see their devoted attention in a quick turn of the head as we make a sound that interests them. They yearn to understand, to perceive, and this trait forms the basis of the relationship we create with them. We know the importance of trying to "read the dog," but equally important is the dog's attempt at reading us, and that cocked head indicates the extent to which they will go to try to understand our humble efforts at communicating with them.

DOG HUMOR

Do dogs have a sense of humor?
It's hard to avoid that conclusion watching
them construct spontaneous games with each
other for the sheer delight and joy of it.

Seeing playful mischief arise in one dog as it pulls a prank on another should fill us with delight. What sort of creature is this that can interact with life so joyously? Dogs may not do stand-up comedy, but they creatively express the comic in their own context, leaving us to respond with a hearty laugh.

THE REPENTANT DOG

Dogs have few scruples about
                    expressing sorrow and regret.

While in the aftermath of stealing our sandwich they may give us a wide berth to allow our emotions to cool down, they have a completely straightforward and natural manner about trying to patch things up once an appropriate time has passed. This is most often expressed through proximity: a lick, a nudge, soliciting assurance that the broader context of the relationship has not been lost.

DAILY REBIRTH

Devotion elicits awe.

How moving to see an elderly dog, stiff and arthritic, suddenly come back to life when its owner greets it on coming home from work. Not a trace of scolding or shame – just pure joy – joy that communicates its understanding through delicious licks and excited yips. It is a veritable rebirth, if even for a few short minutes, before the dog collapses once again on its dog bed, incapable of any more antics. No matter. In that one shimmering moment, years of companionship reveal a trust so complete that one need never wonder why dogs have so captured our imaginations, filling our hearts to overflowing.

THE FLEXIBLE DOG

Dogs deal with moodiness in ways we can learn from.

Above all, they shift gracefully from moment to moment, keeping things upbeat and focused outside of themselves. Talk about flexibility! Rarely do they seem to give in to excessive self-pity, but instead are continuously captivated by the sheer naturalness and magic of the world. Such interest and fascination are a tonic for life, an antidote to the troubling feelings that come from never being able to get beyond your nose.

FIDELITY

Disloyalty is not a trait found
in the lexicon of a dog.

Once a bond is formed, they are ever seeking
ways to express devotion, whether with the
simplicity of an affectionate lick when we're
feeling down, or the protective growl as a
stranger approaches during a late-night
walk. They don't abandon us after a disagreement or fail to make up
after a stern correction. They always live with the broader picture, and
their behavior reinforces a deeper truth that is so rare in our human
relationships: that there is no limit to genuine fidelity and friendship.
In a world that has become cynical about long-term commitments,
that is no small wonder.

THE FINAL STEP

One of the most serious responsibilities we assume
when caring for a dog is developing the wisdom to
know when to help them end their lives with dignity.

How can there not be tears and hesitation when
our memories sort through a lifetime of love
and affection? Nevertheless, our dogs cannot
understand and find meaning in their suffering,
and they trust us to have their best interests in
mind, even when it means making a final
decision. Listen to your dog. Your dog will
intuitively know when it's time, and his eyes
will plead with you to take this step. Compassion
here involves a responsiveness that transcends
our own ego-centered feelings.

" 'To the Lord belong the earth and all it contains…' O God, enlarge within us the sense of fellowship with all living things, our brethren the animals to whom You have given the earth as their home in common with us. May we realize that they live, not for us alone, but for themselves and for You, and that they love the sweetness of life."

~ *The Liturgy of St. Basil*

ABOUT THE MONKS OF NEW SKETE

 The Monks of New Skete are an Eastern Orthodox monastic community living in Cambridge, New York. They began in 1966 and support themselves by breeding and training dogs at their monastery, and by making and selling speciality foods. They are the authors of *Divine Canine, In the Spirit of Happiness: Spiritual Wisdom for Living, I & Dog, Rise Up With a Listening Heart*, and their best-selling guides to dog training, *How to Be Your Dog's Best Friend* and *The Art of Raising a Puppy*. For additional information, visit their website at www.newsketemonks.com

ACKNOWLEDGMENTS

The text of this book was inspired by all the dogs we live with, work with and have known, and by the stunning photography provided by Mark Asher. We are very grateful for his participation in this project. Thanks also to photographers Monique Stauder, Katrina Lohr and Vincent Remini for supplying some additional beautiful photos.

As always, we enjoy the process of creating books with our agent and editor Kate Hartson and our favorite book designer, Tina Taylor. We also want to acknowledge our friends at Hyperion: Executive Editor Brenda Copeland and her assistant Kate Griffin, and all those who've taken great care in preparing this book for publication, Navorn Johnson, Shubhani Sarkar, David Lott—thank you all!